RUSSIAN SWEARING:

*104 Swearing Russian Verbs Conjugated
in All Tenses with Examples*

By
Nikolai Nikolsky and Liz Bryant

Table of Contents

v

Ахуеть (от охуеть)

1) to be really surprised

2) to exceed, go beyond the limit

Future

Я ахуею	Мы ахуеем
Ты ахуеешь	Вы ахуеете
Он ахуеет	Они ахуеют

Past

Он ахуел

Она ахуела

Они ахуели

Adverb

-

Directive

-

Examples:

Я просто ахуел, когда допёр, что меня действительно выгнали с работы насовсем. I was really fucking shocked when I wised up I had really been given the air for good.

Да этот парень совсем ахуел, не понимает где свои, а где чужие. Well, this guy is really off his fucking limits, he doesn't get who's friend or foe.

Блядов**а**ть (спать со всеми подряд, изменять)

1) To be unfaithful, to behave like a slut, to prostitute, to have promiscuous sex

Present

Я бляд**у**ю	Мы бляд**у**ем
Ты блядуешь	Вы блядуете
Он блядует	Они блядуют

Past

Он блядов**а**л

Она блядов**а**ла

Они блядов**а**ли

Adverb

Блядуя

Directive

Блядуй

Блядуйте

Examples:

Все 15 лет брака муж блядовал по-страшному, а как заболел, так сразу жена – самая лучшая. During all the 15 years of marriage the husband's been fucking around, but when he got sick, he was like – my wife's the best.

Блядовать много ума не надо, а вот верного мужика днём с огнём теперь не сыщешь. It doesn't take much to fuck around, but you can't find a faithful man in daylight even with a flashlight.

Въеб**а**ть (1)ударить кого-то, 2)выпить)

1)To kick the shit out of someone
2)To knock back (as in a drink)

Въеб**а**ть(ся) (**удариться, об автомобиле**)

1) To hit/damage

Future

Я въеб**у**(сь)	Мы въеб**ё**м(ся)
Ты въеб**ё**шь(ся)	Вы въеб**ё**те(сь)
Он въеб**ё**т(ся)	Они въеб**у**т(ся)

Past   Adverb

Он въеб**а**л(ся)   –

Она въеб**а**ла(сь)

Они въеб**а**ли(сь)   **Directive**
                    Въеб**и**
                    Въеб**и**те

Examples:

Он въбал ему в лицо.   He fucking hit him in the face.

Полицейский сильно въебал преступнику.   The policeman fucking hit the criminal.

Въебала свою BMW прямо в дерево! She fucking ran her BMW straight into the tree!

Въебали по пиву.   We fucking hit some beers.

Выебать

1) To screw, to fuck

2) To fuck up (someone)

Future

Я выебу	Мы выебем
Ты выебешь	Вы выебете
Он выебет	Они выебут

Past

Он выебал

Она выебала

Они выебали

Adverb

–

Directive

Выеби

Выебите

Examples:

Преподаватель выебал мне все мозги. The teacher fucked up my brain.

Старшие ребята серьёзно выебут меня за этот проступок. The older guys would fuck me up for this offence.

Просто выеби её и забудь. Just fuck her and forget about it.

Выебу всех вас! I will fuck up all of you!

Выёбываться (много строить из себя, выпендриваться)

1) to fuck around, to show off

Present

Я выёбываюсь	Мы выёбываемся
Ты выёбываешься	Вы выёбываетесь
Он выёбывается	Они выёбываются

Past

Он (до)выёбывался

Она (до)выёбывалась

Они (до)выёбывались

Adverb

Выёбываясь

Directive

-

Examples:

Я не понимаю, перед кем ты сейчас выёбываешься? I can't really understand in fron of who you're fucking showing off?

Ну что, довыёбывалась, подружка? Теперь будешь год ездить на метро. So what, no more fucking around, my dear friend? You'll have to use the tube for a year now.

Вылизать

1) Clean smth really well, lick clean
2) To lick all over
3) Correct to a dot

Present

Я в**ы**лижу	Мы в**ы**лижем
Ты в**ы**лижешь	Вы в**ы**лижете
Он в**ы**лижет	Они в**ы**лижут

Past

Он в**ы**лизал

Она в**ы**лизала

Они в**ы**лизали

Adverb

—

Directive

В**ы**лижи

В**ы**лижите

Examples:

Этот извращенец вылизал мне все пальцы ног. This pervert licked my toes all over.

Квартира к нашем приезду была идеально вылизана. By the time of our arrival the apartment was licked clean.

Вы́срать(ся)

1) To shit, to take a dump, to crap
2) To finally do smth
3) Say smth, blurt out

Future

Я вы́сру(сь)	Мы вы́срем(ся)
Ты вы́срешь(ся)	Вы вы́срете(сь)
Он вы́срет(ся)	Они вы́срут(ся)

Past

Он вы́срал(ся)

Она вы́срала(сь)

Они вы́срали(сь)

Adverb

–

Directive

Вы́сри(сь)

Вы́срите(сь)

Examples:

Сегодня я высрал огромную какашку. I shit a giant turd today.

Наконец-то мы высрали хотя бы десять страниц доклада. Finally we've shit out at least 10 pages of the report.

Давай, постарайся высрать из себя хоть какое-то достойное оправдание. Come on, try fucking make up at least some decent explanation.

Прежде чем высрать какую-то хрень, лучше сначала два раза подумать. Before fucking blurting out some damn nonsense, you better think twice.

Выссать

1) To pee smth out

Future

Я выссу	Мы выссым
Ты выссышь	Вы выссыте
Он выссыт	Они выссут

Past

Он выссал

Она выссала

Они выссали

Adverb

–

Directive

Выссы

Выссыте

Examples:

Если я выпью буквально пару бутылок пива, то потом выссу всю воду из организма. If I drink just a couple of bottles of beer, I will then piss out all the liquid from my body.

В**ы**трахать

1) To fuck, bang, screw

Future

Я в**ы**трахаю	Мы в**ы**трахаем
Ты в**ы**трахаешь	Вы в**ы**трахаете
Он в**ы**трахает	Они в**ы**трахают

Past   ### Adverb

Он в**ы**трахал   –

Она в**ы**трахала   ### Directive

Они в**ы**трахали   –

                       –

Examples:

Спорим, что я вытрахаю её до потери сознания. I bet I'll fuck her till she faints.

Да за две недели он вытрахал пол деревни! In two weeks he fucked half the village!

Говн**и**ться (вредничать, упираться)

1) To be a hard ass, not to be eager to do smth

Present

Я	говн**ю**сь	Мы	говн**и**мся
Ты	говн**и**шься	Вы	говн**и**тесь
Он	говн**и**тся	Они	говн**я**тся

Past   **Adverb**

Он говн**и**лся   –

Она говн**и**лась   **Directive**

Они говн**и**лись   –

Examples:

Я не хочу ничего у него спрашивать, потому что он всегда говнится и портит мне настроение. I don't want to ask him anything, because he always is a hard ass and I don't want to flag my spirits.

По какому поводу говнишься? Что тебя не устраивает? Why are you being such a hard ass? What is it that you aren't happy with?

Дать пизды (побить кого-то (то же, что и «отпиздить»; отругать (чаще употребляется в этом значении))

1) to beat up, to trash.
2) to wipe hell out of smbd., burn up, scold, ream somebody's ass out

Present

Я да**ю** пизд**ы**	Мы да**ём** пизд**ы**
Ты да**ёшь** пизд**ы**	Вы да**ёте** пизд**ы**
Он да**ёт** пизд**ы**	Они да**ют** пизд**ы**

Past   ### Adverb

Он д**а**л пизд**ы**	–
Она дал**а** пизд**ы**	**Directive**
Они д**а**ли пизд**ы**	Дай пизд**ы**
	Дайте пизд**ы**

Examples:

Ребята, нам надо собраться и закончить этот проект, иначе в понедельник шеф нам всем даст пизды. Guys, we need to organize ourselves and finish the project, if not the boss will kick our asses out on Monday.

Я видел его лицо после той драки. Ему дали серьёзной пизды. I saw his face after that fight. They fucked him up quite bad.

(С) Дéлать минéт

1) To perform oral sex on a man, give a blow job

Present

Я дéлаю минет	Мы дéлаем минет
Ты дéлаешь минет	Вы дéлаете минет
Он дéлает минет	Они дéлают минет

Future

Я сдéлаю минет	Мы сдéлаем минет
Ты сдéлаешь минет	Вы сдéлаете минет
Он сдéлает минет	Они сдéлают минет

Past

Он (с)дéлал минет

Она (с)дéлала минет

Они (с)дéлал минет

Adverb

Дéлая минет

Directive

(С)дéлай минет

(С)дéлайте минет

Examples:

Потом я попросил её сделать мне минет.   Then I asked her for a blow job.

Пока она делала мне минет, я думал, что усну. I thought I would fall asleep when she was giving me a blow job.

Додроч**и**ть

1) To finish masturbating, to finish jerking off,

Future

Я додроч**у**	Мы додр**о**чим
Ты додр**о**чишь	Вы додр**о**чите
Он додр**о**чит	Они додр**о**чат

Past

Он додроч**и**л

Она додроч**и**ла

Они додроч**и**ли

Adverb

–

Directive

Додроч**и**

Додроч**и**те

Examples:

После того как она мне додрочила, интерес у неё совсем пропал. After she finished jerking me off, she lost all of her interest.

Настроение испортилось, но додрочить всё же хотелось. The mood was spoiled, but I still needed to finish jerking off.

Доеб**а**ть (ся)

1) To screw/fuck till the end/ finish fucking

2) To get on somebody's nerves

Future

Я доеб**у**(сь)   Мы доеб**ё**м(ся)

Ты доеб**ё**шь(ся)   Вы доеб**ё**те(сь)

Он доеб**ё**т(ся)   Они доеб**у**т(ся)

Past   ### Adverb

Он доеб**а**л(ся)   –

Она доеб**а**ла(сь)   ### Directive

Они доеб**а**ли(сь)   Доеб**и**(сь)

                             Доеб**и**те(сь)

Examples:

Доебался до меня по поводу моего опоздания.   He fucked with me because I came late.

Опять будет доёбываться со своими отчётами.   And again he'll be fucking getting on my nerves with his reports.

Доебал тёлочку и свалил.   Finished fucking the hot chick and got away.

Ну мы доебались, теперь придётся бороться с последствиями. So we're done fucking, now we'll have to deal with the consequences.

Допереть (дойти до чего-то, сообразить; добраться куда-то после долгого пути)

1) to understand

2) to get somewhere

Future

Я допру(сь)   Мы допрём(ся)

Ты допрёшь(ся)   Вы допрёте(сь)

Он допрёт(ся)   Они допрут(ся)

Past   ### Adverb

Он допёр(ся)   –

Она допёрла(сь)   ### Directive

Они допёрли(сь)   Допри(сь)

                      Доприте(сь)

Examples:

Ну наконец-то ты допёр! А то я уж подумал, что ты полный дебил! Finally you get it! Because I was already thinking you're a complete morron!

Я что-то никак не допру, как правильно решается эта задача. I can't get how to solve this problem.

Допизд**е**ться (договориться до чего-то, сболтнуть лишнего)

1) to agree on smth

2) to talk too much

Future

Я допизж**у**сь	Мы допизд**и**мся
Ты допизд**и**шься	Вы допизд**и**тесь
Он допизд**и**тся	Они допизд**я**тся

Past

Он допизд**е**лся

Она досдопизд**е**лась

Они допизд**е**лись

Adverb

–

Directive

Допизд**и**сь

Допизд**и**тесь

Examples:

Ну всё друг, ты допизделся. Сейчас я тебя научу держать язык за зубами. You've fucking talked too much. I'll teach ya to keep your mouth shut.

В итоге, допизделись до того, что решили рвануть на Новый Год в Азию с палатками. As a result, we fucking agreed to go to Asia for the New Year, and with tents.

Доср**а**ть(ся)

1) To finish taking a crap, to finish pooping

2) To fight (not physically)

Future

Я досру(сь)	Мы досрём(ся)
Ты досрёшь(ся)	Вы досрёте(сь)
Он досрёт(ся)	Они досрут(ся)

Past   **Adverb**

Он досрал(ся)   –

Она досрала(сь)   **Directive**

Они досрали(сь)   Досри(сь)

                          Досрите(сь)

Examples:

Они досрались до такой степени, что просто уже не могли видеть друг друга. They've been fighting so hard they couldn't stand each other any longer.

Дай мне спокойно досрать, я тебе потом перезвоню. Just let me finish my shit here in peace, and I'll call you back.

Надеюсь, что мы все-таки не досрёмся до развода. I hope that we won't fucking fight ourselves to a divorce.

Вечно так: только досру, как уже и перерыв заканчивается. It's always the same story: as soon as I finish taking a shit, the break's already ending.

Досс**ать**

1) To finish peeing

Future

Я досс**у**	Мы досс**ым**
Ты досс**ы**шь	Вы досс**ы**те
Он досс**ы**т	Они досс**у**т

Past	**Adverb**
Он досс**а**л	–
Она досс**а**ла	**Directive**
Они досс**а**ли	Досс**ы**
	Досс**ы**те

Examples:

Так, девочки, быстренько доссали и валите отсюда, нам тут надо поговорить. OK girls, come one, finish pissing and get the hell outta here, we need to talk.

С трудом могу доссать, мучают резкие боли. I can hardly finish pissing, I have some really sharp pains.

Дроч**и**ть(ся)

1) To masturbate, to jerk off

2) To be doing smth for a long time, to fuck with smth

Present

Я дроч**у**(сь)	Мы др**о**чим(ся)
Ты др**о**чишь(ся)	Вы др**о**чите(сь)
Он др**о**чит(ся)	Они др**о**чат(ся)

Past

Он дроч**и**л(ся)

Она дроч**и**ла(сь)

Они дроч**и**ли(сь)

Adverb

Дроч**а**(сь)

Directive

Дроч**и**(сь)

Дроч**и**те(сь)

Examples:

Уже неделю дрочусь с этой дурацкой программой. I've been fucking with this software for a week now.

Дрочить надо каждый день. One should jerk off every day.

Он дрочил фотографии обнажённых голливудских звёзд найденные на интернете. He jerked off to pictures of naked Hollywood stars he found online.

Она методично дрочит мне мозг. She methodically fucks with my brains.

Еб**а**ть (ся)

1) To fuck (literally and with somebody's brain)

Present

Я еб**у**	Мы еб**ё**м
Ты еб**ё**шь	Вы еб**ё**те
Он еб**ё**т	Они еб**у**т

Past

Он еб**а**л

Она еб**а**ла

Они еб**а**ли

Adverb

Еб**я**

Directive

Еб**и**

Еб**и**те

Examples:

Он ебал ее два часа.	He fucked her for two hours.
Он часто ебет мне мозги.	He often fucks with me.
Мы ебались в первый раз.	We were fucking for the first time.
Ебал я вас всех!	Fuck you all!

Задроч**и**ть(ся)

1) To masturbate, to jack off, to jerk off

2) To get tired of smth, to be fucking with smth for a long time

Present

Я задроч**у**(сь)	Мы задр**о**чим(ся)
Ты задр**о**чишь(ся)	Вы задр**о**чите(сь)
Он задр**о**чит(ся)	Они задр**о**чат(ся)

Past

Он задроч**и**л(ся)

Она задроч**и**ла(сь)

Они задроч**и**ли(сь)

Adverb

–

Directive

Задроч**и**(сь)

Задроч**и**те(сь)

Examples:

Я задрочился уже с этим эссе. Пойду лучше спать. I'm tired of fucking with this essay. I better go get some sleep.

Задрочила мне весь мозг своим нытьём. She just fucked my brain up with her nagging.

Затем она взяла в руки мой хуй и активно его задрочила. The she got my dick in her hands and startend jacking me off.

Заеб**а**ть (ся)

1) To get on someone's nerves/to be sick of someone

Future

Я заеб**у**(сь)   Мы заеб**ё**м(ся)

Ты заеб**ё**шь(ся)   Вы заеб**ё**те(сь)

Он заеб**ё**т(ся)   Они заеб**у**т(ся)

Past   ### Adverb

Он заеб**а**л(ся)   –

Она заеб**а**ла(сь)   ### Directive

Они заеб**а**ли(сь)   Заеб**и**(сь)

                          Заеб**и**те(сь)

Examples:

Как же ты меня заебал!   I'm fucking sick of you!

Этот парень заебёт кого угодно. This guy can fucking get on anyone's nerves.

Заеб**а**шить (сделать что-то)

1) to perform an action (quickly)

Future

Я заеб**а**шу	Мы заеб**а**шим
Ты заеб**а**шишь	Вы заеб**а**шите
Он заеб**а**шит	Они заеб**а**шут

Past   **Adverb**

Он заеб**а**шил   –

Она заеб**а**шила   **Directive**

Они заеб**а**шили   Заеб**а**шь

Заеб**а**шьте

Examples:

Заебашу классный лук с этим новым свитером. I will fucking make a cool look with this new sweater.

Заебашим по стаканчику рома? Let's fucking knock back a shot of rum?

Засос**а**ть(ся)

1) to French kiss (literally to suck)

2) to suck in

Future

Я засос**у**(сь)	Мы засос**ё**м(ся)
Ты засос**ё**шь(ся)	Вы засос**ё**те(сь)
Он засос**ё**т(ся)	Они засос**у**т(ся)

Past

Он засос**а**л(ся)

Она засос**а**ла(сь)

Они засос**а**ли(сь)

Adverb

–

Directive

Засос**и**(сь)

Засос**и**те(сь)

Examples:

Во время медленного танца эта парочка засосалась, как в первый раз. During the slow dance this couple started to French kiss as if it was for the first time.

Засосала как пылесос.   Sucked it in like a vacuum.

Засра**ть**(ся)

1) To shit all over (figuratively and literally)

Future

Я заср**у**(сь)	Мы заср**ё**м(ся)
Ты заср**ё**шь(ся)	Вы заср**ё**те(сь)
Он заср**ё**т(ся)	Они заср**у**т(ся)

Past   Adverb

Past	Adverb
Он засра**л**(ся)	-
Она засра**ла**(сь)	**Directive**
Они засра**ли**(сь)	Заср**и**(сь)
	Заср**и**те(сь)

Examples:

Они мне все мозги засрали своими высказываниями. They've shit all over my mind with their statements

Собака засрала всю квартиру. The dog shit all over the apartment.

Засс**а**ть

1) to chicken out

2) to piss all over smth

Future

Я засс**у**	Мы засс**ы**м
Ты засс**ы**шь	Вы засс**ы**те
Он засс**ы**т	Они засс**у**т

Past

Он засс**а**л

Она засс**а**ла

Они засс**а**ли

Adverb

—

Directive

Засс**ы**

Засс**ы**те

Examples:

Да, после нашего последнего предупреждения, он, похоже, серьёзно зассал. Yeah, seems like after our last warning he really chickened out.

У ребёнка недержание. Опять зассал всю постель. The kid has incontinence. He's pissed all over the bed again.

А не зассышь с нами ночью на кладбище пойти? Won't you chicken out to go with us to the cemetery at night?

Надоел этот грёбаный кот! Зассал всё вокруг: диван, пол, стулья. I'm tired of this fucking cat! He's pissed over everything: the sofa, the floor, the chairs.

Затр**а**хать(ся)

1) to fuck, bang, screw

2) to get tired of smth

3) to bother, to fuck up, to piss off, be a nuisance, to get on somebody's nerves

Future

Я затр**а**хаю(сь)   Мы затр**а**хаем(ся)

Ты затр**а**хаешь(ся)   Вы затр**а**хаете(сь)

Он затр**а**хает(ся)   Они затр**а**хают(ся)

Past   ### Adverb

Он затр**а**хал(ся)   –

Она затр**а**хала(сь)   ### Directive

Они затр**а**хали(сь)   Затр**а**хай(ся)

Затр**а**хайте(сь)

Examples:

Я сегодня жутко затрахался на работе. I'm so fucking tired after today's work.

Ты меня уже вконец затрахал со своими проблемами! You've really fucking made me sick of hearing about your problems!

Затрахаю тебя до полусмерти. I will fuck your brains out.

Как же ты всех затрахала! Everyone is so fucking sick of you! (Literally, how much you have fucked everyone)

Захуя́рить (сделать что-то)

1) to do smth

Future

Я захуя́рю	Мы захуя́рим
Ты захуя́ришь	Вы захуя́рите
Он захуя́рит	Они захуя́рят

Past

Он захуя́рил

Она захуя́рила

Они захуя́рили

Adverb

–

Directive

Захуя́рь

Захуя́рьте

Examples:

Сейчас быстренько захуярю супчик, и будет отличный обед. I'll go fucking make a soup now really quickly and we'll have a fucking awesome lunch.

Не помню, куда захуярил свой фотоаппарат. Теперь придётся просить у кого-нибудь. Don't remember where I put my fucking photo camera. Will have to ask someone to borrow me one.

Изъеб**а**ться (также "изъебнуться": делать что-то с большими усилиями)

1) to make a big effort

Future

Я изъеб**у**сь	Мы изъеб**ё**мся
Ты изъеб**ё**шься	Вы изъеб**ё**тесь
Он изъеб**ё**тся	Они изъеб**у**тся

Past   ### Adverb

Он изъеб**а**лся   –

Она изъеб**а**лась   ### Directive

Они изъеб**а**лись   Изъеб**и**сь

                         Изъеб**и**тесь

Examples:

Я как-то <u>изъебнулся</u> и смог-таки достать упавший за холодильник телефон. I fucking outdid myself and got that phone from behind the fridge.

Я изъебался искать нормальный отель на рождественские праздники – цены безумные! I fucking outdid myself having to look for a normal hotel for Christmas holidays – prices are crazy high!

Лиз**а**ть(ся)

1) To lick
2) To kiss, to smooch
3) To eat pussy

Present

Я лиж**у**(сь)	Мы л**и**жем(ся)
Ты л**и**жешь(ся)	Вы л**и**жете(сь)
Он л**и**жет(ся)	Они л**и**жут(ся)

Past

Он лиз**а**л(ся)

Она лиз**а**ла(сь)

Они лиз**а**ли(сь)

Adverb

–

Directive

Лиж**и**(сь)

Лиж**и**те(сь)

Examples:

В этом клубе до туалета спокойно не дойти, просто противно: в холле все вечно лижутся. In this club it's not that easy to reach the toilet, it's just disgusting: everyone's always fucking smooching in the hallway.

Он большой любитель лизать киски. He's a big fan of eating out pussies.

Взяла себе два шарика шоколадного мороженого. Лизала его и радовалась. Got myself two scoops of chocolate ice-cream. I was licking it feeling happy.

Этот придурок вечно лижет всем жопу, никакого самоуважения. This jerk always licks everyone's ass, no self-respect at all.

Наеб**а**ть (обмануть)

1) to screw someone over, to con, to fuck someone over

Present

Я на**ё**бываю	Мы на**ё**бываем
Ты на**ё**бываешь	Вы на**ё**бываете
Он на**ё**бывает	Они на**ё**бывают

Past   Adverb

Он наеб**а**л   -

Она наеб**а**ла   **Directive**

Они наеб**а**ли   -

Examples:

Этот гандон наебал меня на штуку баксов! This douche bag fucked me over for a thousand bucks!

Ты меня не наебёшь - я сам кого хочешь наебу. You won't fuck me over - I myself can fuck anyone over if I want to.

Наебну**ть**ся (споткунтсья, упасть и удариться)

1) to fall down and hurt oneself

Future

Я наебн**у**сь	Мы наебн**ё**мся
Ты наебн**ё**шься	Вы наебн**ё**тесь
Он наебн**ё**тся	Они наебн**у**тся

Past   ## Adverb

Он наебн**у**лся   -

Она наебн**у**лась   ## Directive

Они наебн**у**лись   Наебн**и**сь

                          Наебн**и**тесь

Examples:

Смотрите не наебнитесь – тут очень скользко. Be careful not to fucking fall – it's really slippery here.

Я вчера сильно наебнулся на лестнице. Моя задница теперь – сплошной синяк. I had a really nasty fucking fall yesterday on the stairs. My ass is bruised.

Напердеть

1) To have farted, to fart

Future

Я наперж**у**	Мы наперд**и**м
Ты наперд**и**шь	Вы наперд**и**те
Он наперд**и**т	Они наперд**я**т

Past   ### Adverb

Он наперд**е**л   -

Она наперд**е**ла   **Directive**

Они наперд**е**ли   Наперд**и**

                Наперд**и**те

Examples:

Дети придумали дурацкое развлечение – напердеть в пакет и нюхать. The kids invented a stupid game – fart in a bag and then smell it.

Боже мой, ты что - напердел? Такое впечатление, что здесь кто-то умер! Oh my God, have you just farted? It seems like someone died in here!

Насрать (опорожниться)

1) to take a shit

Future

Я насру	Мы насрём
Ты насрёшь	Вы насрёте
Он насрёт	Они насрут

Past

Он насрал

Она насрала

Они насрали

Adverb

-

Directive

Насри

Насрите

Examples:

Пойду-ка насру кучу! I'll go take a shit.

Собачка такая маленькая, а насрала, как медведь. This doggy is so tiny, but it shit like a bear.

Наху**я**читься (чего-то употребить, наесться, напиться)

1) get wasted on something, eat to much or drink too much (usually alcohol)

Future

Я наху**я**чусь	Мы наху**я**чимся
Ты наху**я**чишься	Вы наху**я**читесь
Он наху**я**чится	Они наху**я**чатся

Past   ### Adverb

Он наху**я**чился   –

Она наху**я**чилась   **Directive**

Они наху**я**чились   Наху**я**чься

Наху**я**чьтесь

Examples:

Вчера так нахуячился, сегодня просто умираю. Yesterday I got so fucking wasted, today I'm feeling like a dead man.

Его любимое занятие: нахуячиться водки в субботу и проспать до вечера воскресенья. His favorite is to get fucking wasted on vodka on Saturday and then sleep until Sunday night.

Обдроч**и**ть(ся)

1) To jerk off all over something

2) To wear something down

Future

Я обдроч**у**(сь)	Мы обдр**о**чим(ся)
Ты обдр**о**чишь(ся)	Вы обдр**о**чите(сь)
Он обдр**о**чит(ся)	Они обдр**о**чат(ся)

Past

Он обдроч**и**л(ся)

Она обдроч**и**ла(сь)

Они обдроч**и**ли(сь)

Adverb

–

Directive

Обдроч**и**(сь)

Обдроч**и**те(сь)

Examples:

Глядя эту порнуху хочется просто обдрочиться. Watching this porn just makes you wanna jerk it all off.

Чувствую, что весь обдрочусь, пока буду ждать. I fell like I'll jerk off while I'll be waiting.

Он обдрочил весь компьютер. He jerked off all over his computer.

Обосра́ть(ся)

1) To trash talk

2) To shit oneself

3) To be scared

Future

Я обосру́(сь)	Мы обосрём(ся)
Ты обосрёшь(ся)	Вы обосрёте(сь)
Он обосрёт(ся)	Они обосру́т(ся)

Past   ### Adverb

Он обосра́л(ся)   -

Она обосра́ла(сь)   ### Directive

Они обосра́ли(сь)   Обосри́(сь)

Обосри́те(сь)

Examples:

Почему ты всё время обсираешь мои идеи? Why do you always fucking trash my ideas?

Обосрал весь унитаз и не смыл за собой. He shit all over the toilet and didn't flush his shit.

Обосрать легко. А ты придумай сам что-нибудь! It's easy to just shit all over something. But try to come up with something yourself!

Обосс**а**ть (ся)

1) To wet/piss on someone

Future

Я обосс**у**	Мы обосс**ы**м
Ты обосс**ы**шь	Вы обосс**ы**те
Он обосс**ы**т	Они обосс**у**т

Past

Он обосс**а**л

Она обосс**а**ла

Они обосс**а**ли

Adverb

−

Directive

Обосс**ы**

Обосс**ы**те

Examples:

У тебя такое лёгкое домашнее задание. Сделать его — как два пальца обоссать. You have a very easy homework assignment. Doing it is easy as pissing on two fingers.

В общественном туалете всегда кто-нибудь уже успел обоссать весь пол. In a public toilet someone always has already pissed all over the floor.

Обосс**а**ться

1) To wet, to pee, to piss oneself

2) To wet yourself (when something is really funny)

Future

Я обосс**у**сь	Мы обосс**ы**мся
Ты обосс**ы**шься	Вы обосс**ы**тесь
Он обосс**ы**тся	Они обосс**у**тся

Past

Он обосс**а**лся

Она обосс**а**лась

Они обосс**а**лись

Adverb

–

Directive

Обосс**ы**сь

Обосс**ы**тесь

Examples:

Ты уже большой парень, тебе 5 лет, а ты опять обоссался. You're a big boy already, you're 5 years old, yet you pissed your bed again.

Ты реально обоссышься от смеха, когда услышишь её историю. You'll piss yourself when you hear her story.

Если мы сейчас же не остановимся где-нибудь, то я обоссусь прямо в машине. If we don't make a stop somewhere right now, I will piss myself right in the car.

Не обоссысь от смеха, когда будуешь смотреть это видео. Я даже не знаю, что у этих людей в голове творится. Don't piss yourself laughing when youh watch this video. I don't even know what these people have in their heads.

Объеб**а**ть(ся)

1) To fuck over
2) To get high on drugs

Future

Я объеб**у**(сь)   Мы объеб**ё**м(ся)
Ты объеб**ё**шь(ся)   Вы объеб**ё**те(сь)
Он объеб**ё**т(ся)   Они объеб**у**т(ся)

Past   ### Adverb

Он объеб**а**л(ся)   –

Она объеб**а**ла(сь)   ### Directive

Они объеб**а**ли(сь)   Объеб**и**(сь)
                              Объеб**и**те(сь)

Examples:

Кассирша объеб**а**ла меня со сдачей. The cashier fucked me over with the change.

Объеб**а**ли всю компанию!   Fucked up the whole company!

Мы объеб**а**лись кокса на той вечеринке. We got high on coke (cocaine) in that party.

Тебе меня не объеб**а**ть! You won't fuck me over!

Объеб**о**шить (то же самое, что наебать, но употребляется реже; обыграть или обойти в результатах)

1) to screw someone over, to con, to fuck someone over

Future

Я объеб**о**шу   Мы объеб**о**шим

Ты объеб**о**шишь   Вы объеб**о**шите

Он объеб**о**шит   Они объеб**о**шат

Past   ### Adverb

Он объеб**о**шил   —

Она объеб**о**шила   ### Directive

Они объеб**о**шили   Объеб**о**шь

                     Объеб**о**шьте

Examples:

Этот урод меня опять объебошил в карты. This bastard fucked me over playing cards once again.

Не ходите в этот ресторан. Там вас точно объебошать. Don't go to that restaurant. They will fuck you over for sure.

Остоп**и**здеть (надоесть)

1) to get tired of smth, to get on somebody's nerves.

Future

Я остоп**и**зжу	Мы остоп**и**здим
Ты остоп**и**здишь	Вы остоп**и**здите
Он остоп**и**здит	Они остоп**и**здят

Past | ### Adverb

Он остоп**и**здел   –

Она остоп**и**здела   **Directive**

Они остоп**и**здели   –

Examples:

Мне остопиздел этот Интерент. Скорость отвратительная!
This fucking Internet is getting on my nerves. The speed is terrible!

С таким подходом ты быстро ему остопиздишь и он тебя бросит. With this attitude you'll quickly get him fucking tired of yourself and he'll leave you.

Отлиз**а**ть

1) To eat pussy

Present

Я отлиж**у**	Мы отл**и**жем
Ты отл**и**жешь	Вы отл**и**жете
Он отл**и**жет	Они отл**и**жут

Past   ### Adverb

Он отлиз**а**л   –

Она отлиз**а**ла   ### Directive

Они отлиз**а**ли   Отлиж**и**

                Отлиж**и**те

Examples:

Что касается отлизать, то он в этом деле, похоже, знает толк. As for eating pussy, it seems he knows what he is doing.

Если мужчина никогда не отлизывает, это немного подозрительно. If a guy doesn't ever eat pussy, it's a little suspicious.

Отл**и**ть (пописать)

1) to piss, to take a leak, to urinate,

Future

Я отоль**ю**   Мы отоль**ё**м

Ты отоль**ё**шь   Вы отоль**ё**те

Он отоль**ё**т   Они отоль**ю**т

Past   **Adverb**

Он отл**и**л   —

Она отл**и**л**а**   **Directive**

Они отл**и**л**и**   Отл**е**й

                      Отл**е**йте

Examples:

Да отлейте хотя бы вот в это ведро. Go piss at least in this bucket.

Сейчас отолью и пойдём в супермаркет. Let me just go take a leak and then we'll go to the supermarket.

Отмудохать (избить кого-то, то же, что "отпиздить")

1) to beat up

Future

Я отмудохаю	Мы отмудохаем
Ты отмудохаешь	Вы отмудохаете
Он отмудохает	Они отмудохают

Past

Он отмудохал

Она отмудохала

Они отмудохали

Adverb

-

Directive

Отмудохай

Отмудохайте

Examples:

Я всё расскажу своему брату и он тебя отмудохает! Так что отвали от меня! I'll tell everything to my brother and he'll fucking beat the shit out of you! So back off!

За такое его надо просто отмудохать, чтобы стало понятно, что так не делается. One should fill him in for something like that, so that he would understand that things can't be done this way.

Отосрать

1) To take a shit

Future

Я отосру	Мы отосрём
Ты отосрёшь	Вы отосрёте
Он отосрёт	Они отосрут

Past

Он отосрал

Она отосрала

Они отосрали

Adverb

–

Directive

Отосри

Отосрите

Examples:

Было бы неплохо отосрать, а то у меня уже живот начинает болеть. It would be nice to take a shit, because my stomach is strating to ache.

Если я сейчас не отосру, то мы никуда не поедем. If I don't have a shit right now, we won't go anywhere.

Отпиздить (побить)

1) to beat up

Future

Я отпизжу   Мы отпиздим

Ты отпиздишь   Вы отпиздите

Он отпиздит   Они отпиздят

Past   ### Adverb

Он отпиздил   –

Она отпиздила   ### Directive

Они отпиздили   Отпизди

                Отпиздите

Examples:

Он опять отпиздил свою жену. Я не понимаю, почему она не напишет на него заявление в полицию. He fucking beat the shit out of his wife again. Can't understand why she doesn't file a police report.

Они сказали мне, что отпиздят меня, если не скажу им, кто это сделал. They said they would fucking beat me up if I didn't tell them who had done it.

Отсос**а**ть

1) To blow, suck off

Future

Я отсос**у**　　　　Мы отсос**ё**м
Ты отсос**ё**шь　　　Вы отсос**ё**те
Он отсос**ё**т　　　Они отсос**у**т

Past　　　　　### Adverb

Он отсос**а**л　　　—

Она отсос**а**ла　　### Directive

Они отсос**а**ли　　Отсос**и**
　　　　　　　　　Отсос**и**те

Examples:

На той точке шлюхи отсосут всего лишь за 20 баксов. In that zone the whores can blow you for just 20 bucks.

Она неплохо отсосала, видимо, опытная. She did suck it off really nicely, seems like she's got some experience.

Оттр**а**хать(ся)

1) To fuck, bang, screw

Future

Я оттр**а**хаю	Мы оттр**а**хаем
Ты оттр**а**хаешь	Вы оттр**а**хаете
Он оттр**а**хает	Они оттр**а**хают

Past

Он оттр**а**хал(ся)

Она оттр**а**хала(сь)

Они оттр**а**хали(сь)

Adverb

–

Directive

Оттр**а**хай

Оттр**а**хайте

Examples:

Не каждому везёт оттрахать такую горячую тёлочку. Not everyone turns out so lucky to fuck such a hot chick.

Оттрахаю тебя до полусмерти, малышка. I will fuck your brains out, baby!

Все только обещают оттрахать хорошенько, а на деле – полные нули. Everyone just brags about giving me a good fuck, but in reality they can't do much.

Отху**я**рить (побить, то же, что «отпиздить»; что-то выполнить/отработать)

1) to beat, to beat the shit out of

2) to complete a project/a job

Future

Я отху**я**рю	Мы отху**я**рим
Ты отху**я**ришь	Вы отху**я**рите
Он отху**я**ришь	Они отху**я**рят

Past

Он отху**я**рил

Она отху**я**рила

Они отху**я**рили

Adverb

–

Directive

Отху**я**рь

Отху**я**рьте

Examples:

Отхуярил два года в ночную смену. Теперь вот здоровье ни к чёрту. Been fucking slaving night shifts for two years. My health's not worth a damn now.

Я тебя сейчас так отхуярю, придурок, что ты забудешь как тебя зовут! I will fucking beat the shit out of you now so that you'll forget your own name.

Отху**я**чить (то же, что отхуярить; оттрахать)

1) to beat, to beat the crap out, to hit

2) to complete a project/a job

3) to fuck

Future

Я отху**я**чу	Мы отху**я**чим
Ты отху**я**чишь	Вы отху**я**чите
Он отху**я**чит	Они отху**я**чат

Past   **Adverb**

Он отху**я**чил   –

Она отху**я**чила   **Directive**

Они отху**я**чили   Отху**я**чь

                            Отху**я**чьте

Examples:

Пацаны, отхуячьте-ка его. Пусть поймёт, кто тут босс. Guys, fucking beat the shit out of him, so that he understands who's the boss around here.

Осталось отхуячить три дня, и начнется отпуск. Three days left to fucking complete this work, and the vacation shall begin.

Охер**е**ть (сильно удивиться чему-то; перейти все границы дозволенного)

1) be very surprised

2) to overstep the boundaries, to go far, go nuts

Future

Я охер**е**ю	Мы охер**е**ем
Ты охер**е**ешь	Вы охер**е**ете
Он охер**е**ет	Они охер**е**ют

Past   ### Adverb

Он охер**е**л	–
Она охер**е**ла	**Directive**
Они охер**е**ли	–

Examples:

Ты охерела совсем! Ты что творишь? You're out of your fucking mind. What the fuck are you doing?

Я совсем охерею, если они в итоге мне не подтвердят кредит. I will be so fucking surprised if they don't confirm my loan.

Охрене**ть** (сильно удивиться чему-то; перейти все границы дозволенного, сойти с ума)

1) be very surprised;

2) to overstep the boundaries, to go far, go nuts

Future

Я охрен**е**ю	Мы охрен**е**ем
Ты охрен**е**ешь	Вы охрен**е**ете
Он охрен**е**ет	Они охрен**е**ют

Past   ### Adverb

Он охрен**е**л	–
Она охрен**е**ла	Directive
Они охрен**е**ли	–

Examples:

Охренеть! Вот это тачка у тебя! Holy shit! Look at that ride you got!

Ты охренел совсем? Куда прёшь! You nuts, man? Where the hell are you going?

Охуев**ать** (быть в шоковом состоянии (несовершенный вид))

1) be (fucking) shocked;

Present

Я охуев**аю**	Мы охуев**аем**
Ты охуев**аешь**	Вы охуев**аете**
Он охуев**ает**	Они охуев**ают**

Past

Он охуев**ал**

Она охуев**ала**

Они охуев**али**

Adverb

Охуев**ая**

Directive

Охуев**ай**

Охуев**айте**

Examples:

Он постоянно охуевал от выходок своей девушки. Она могла не прийди домой ночевать, или могла исчезнуть на три дня без звонка. He'd been fucking living in a permanent state of shock with his girlfriend's behavior. She could not come home for the night, or could disappear for three days without a call.

Я охуеваю от твоего дибилизма. Лучше просто заткнись. I'm so fucking shocked of your stupidity. Just shut up.

Оху**е**ть (быть в шоковом состоянии, то же, что «охуевать», но совершенный вид)

1) be (fucking) shocked;"fuck me!"

Future

Я оху**е**ю	Мы оху**е**ем
Ты оху**е**ешь	Вы оху**е**ете
Он оху**е**ет	Они оху**е**ют

Past   **Adverb**

Он оху**е**л   –

Она оху**е**ла   **Directive**

Они оху**е**ли   –

Examples:

Ты, соска, охуела!   You're fucking nuts, bitch!

Мои родителю охуеют, когда узнают, что меня выгнали из колледжа. My parents will go fucking crazy when they learn I've been kicked out of college.

Отъеб**а**ть(ся)

1) To fuck

2) To leave alone, to fuck off

3) To finish fucking

Future

Я отъеб**у**(сь)	Мы отъеб**ё**мся(ся)
Ты отъеб**ё**шься(ся)	Вы отъеб**ё**тесь(сь)
Он отъеб**ё**тся(ся)	Они отъеб**у**т(ся)

Past

Он отъеб**а**лся(ся)

Она отъеб**а**лась(сь)

Они отъеб**а**ли(сь)

Adverb

Отъеб**а**в

Directive

Отъеб**и**(сь)

Отъеб**и**те(сь)

Examples:

Я тебе давно уже говорил – отъебись от меня, иначе будут проблемы. I've told you a long time ago to fuck off, otherwise you will have problems.

Отъебав жену, я спокойно уснул. Having fucked my wife, I fell asleep quietly.

Сейчас я тебя так отъебу, что не вспомнишь, как тебя зовут. I will now fuck you so hard you won't even remember your name.

Перд**е**ть

1) to fart

Present

Я перж**у**	Мы перд**и**м
Ты перд**и**шь	Вы перд**и**те
Он перд**и**т	Они перд**я**т

Past

Он перд**е**л

Она перд**е**ла

Они перд**е**ли

Adverb

Перд**я**

Directive

Перд**и**

Перд**и**те

Examples:

Неприлично пердеть в обществе других людей, однако же он постоянно это делает. It's impolite to fart in other people's presence, but he constantly does that.

После той похлёбки с фасолью, мы пердели дня три. After having that bean soup we farted for three days.

Передроч**и**ть

1) To masturbate or to jerk off too much, to wack off

Future

Я передроч**у**   Мы передр**о**чим

Ты передр**о**чишь   Вы передр**о**чите

Он передр**о**чит   Они передр**о**чат

Past   Adverb

Он передроч**и**л   –

Она передроч**и**ла   **Directive**

Они передроч**и**ли   Передроч**и**

                    Передроч**и**те

Examples:

Чувствую, что в своё время я передрочил, и теперь предпочитаю просто подождать до встречи с любимой. I fell like back in the old days I just jerked off too much, so now I just prefer to wait till my darling comes back.

Я лучше передрочу, чем буду спать с такой обезьяной. I'll better wack off than fuck such a monkey.

Перееб**а**ть (ся)

1) To fuck

Future

Я перееб**у**(сь)	Мы перееб**ё**мся(ся)
Ты перееб**ё**шься(ся)	Вы перееб**ё**тесь(сь)
Он перееб**ё**тся(ся)	Они перееб**у**т(ся)

Past

Он перееб**а**лся(ся)

Она перееб**а**лась(сь)

Они перееб**а**ли(сь)

Adverb

Перееб**я**

Directive

Перееб**и**(сь)

Перееб**и**те(сь)

Examples:

Переебав уже всех девчонок с кампуса, решили ставить новые цели. Having fucked all the girls from the campus, we decided to set some new goals.

Эта шлюха переебалась уже со всеми моими друзьями. This slut has already fucked all of my friends.

Перепихн**у**ться (совокупиться)

1) to fuck, to get laid

Future

Я перепихн**у**сь	Мы перепихн**ё**мся
Ты перепихн**ё**шься	Вы перепихн**ё**тесь
Он перепихн**ё**тся	Они перепихн**у**тся

Past   ### Adverb

Он перепихн**у**лся   -

Она перепихн**у**лась   **Directive**

Они перепихн**у**лись   Перепихн**и**сь

                              Перепихн**и**тесь

Examples:

Давай по-быстрому перепихнёмся. Let's have a quickie.

Просто перепихнуться мне не интересно. Меня больше интересуют отношения. Just getting laid is not so exciting. I'm more interested in a relationship.

Пересра́ть(ся)

1) To be scared of smth, to be afraid

2) To fight with each other, to quarrel, to argue

Future

Я пересру́(сь)	Мы пересрём(ся)
Ты пересрёшь(ся)	Вы пересрёте(сь)
Он пересрёт(ся)	Они пересру́т(ся)

Past

Он пересра́л(ся)

Она пересра́ла(сь)

Они пересра́ли(сь)

Adverb

–

Directive

Пересри́(сь)

Пересри́те(сь)

Examples:

Я так и знал, что все сначала пересрутся между собой, а только потом начнут слушать мои доводы. I knew that at first everyone would just fucking fight with each other, and only after that they would listen to my arguments.

Оставшись без бензина глубокой ночью на шоссе, мы, честно говоря, немного пересрали. When we were left without gasoline on the highway, deep into the night, frankly speaking, we were scared shitless.

Эта дамочка пересралась уже со всем нашими менеджерами. This lady has already fucking argued with all our managers.

Я, конечно, пересрала, пока открывала конверт с результатами анализов. Of course, I was scared shitless while I was opening the envelope with the test results.

Пересс**а**ть

1) Chicken out, freak out

Future

Я перес**су**	Мы пересс**ы**м
Ты пересс**ы**шь	Вы пересс**ы**те
Он пересс**ы**т	Они перес**су**т

Past　　　　　　　**Adverb**

Он пересс**а**л　　　　–

Она пересс**а**ла　　**Directive**

Они пересс**а**ли　　Пересс**ы**

　　　　　　　　　Пересс**ы**те

Examples:

Лучше два раза пересс**а**ть, чем один раз обосраться. You better chicken out twice, than crap your pants once.

Я тупо перес**с**ал в этой ситуации, такого и врагу не пожелаешь. I completely fucking lost it scared in this situation, you wouldn't wish it on your worst enemy.

Пизда**н**уться (удариться обо что-то; сойти с ума)

1) to hit smth

2) to go crazy, go nuts

Future

Я пизда**н**усь	Мы пизда**н**ёмся
Ты пизда**н**ёшься	Вы пизда**н**ётесь
Он пизда**н**ётся	Они пизда**н**утся

Past   ### Adverb

Он пизда**н**улся	–
Она пизда**н**улась	**Directive**
Они пизда**н**улись	Пизда**н**ись
	Пизда**н**итесь

Examples:

Как же больно я пизданулся об угол стола! I fucking hit the table's corner, it hurts so bad!

Джон совсем пизданулся со своей религией. С ним просто невозможно находиться в одном помещении. John's gotten fucking crazy with his religion. It's impossible to stay in the same room with him.

Пизд**е**ть (поболтать; врать)

1) to chat, to talk

2) to lie

Present

Я пизж**у**   Мы пизд**и**м

Ты пизд**и**шь   Вы пизд**и**те

Он пизд**и**т   Они пизд**я**т

Past   **Adverb**

Он напизд**и**л   —

Она напизд**и**ла   **Directive**

Они напизд**и**ли   Пизд**и**

                          Пизд**и**те

Examples:

Хватит пиздеть! Мне надоели твои сказки! Stop your fucking lies! I'm tired of your fairy-tales!

Попиздили о жизни, выпили бутылку водки. Fucking chatted about life, drank a bottle of vodka.

Пиздить (красть; бить кого-то)

1) to steal, to rob

2) to hit someone, to beat up

Present

Я пизжу	Мы пиздим
Ты пиздишь	Вы пиздите
Он пиздит	Они пиздят

Past   ### Adverb

Он пиздил	–
Она пиздила	**Directive**
Они пиздили	Пизди
	Пиздите

Examples:

Стюардессам запрещено пиздить еду с борта, даже маленькие бутылочки с алкоголем нельзя. Flight-attendants are not allowed to fucking steal food from the planes, not even those small alcohol bottles.

Да тебя пиздить надо, чтобы дурь из башки выбить! One has to fucking beat the shit out of you to straighten out your head!

Пиздоболить (врать)

1) to lie

Present

Я пиздоб**о**лю	Мы пиздоб**о**лим
Ты пиздоб**о**лишь	Вы пиздоб**о**лите
Он пиздоб**о**лит	Они пиздоб**о**лят

Past   ### Adverb

Он пиздоб**о**лил   —

Она пиздоб**о**лила   ### Directive

Они пиздоб**о**лили   —

Examples:

Ты пиздоболишь, я тебе не верю ни капли. You're fucking lying, I don't believe a word of it.

Надо было меньше пиздоболить, потом не пришлось бы оправдываться. You should have lied less, then you wouldn't have to justify yourself.

Пиздова**ть** (куда-то направляться, идити, топать; послать кого-то к такой-то матери)

1) to go somewhere/ to walk somewhere

2) go fuck yourself, get the fuck out of somewhere

Present

Я пизд**у**ю	Мы пизд**у**ем
Ты пизд**у**ешь	Вы пизд**у**ете
Он пизд**у**ет	Они пизд**у**ют

Past   ### Adverb

Он пиздов**а**л   –

Она пиздов**а**ла   ### Directive

Они пиздов**а**ли   Пизд**у**й

Пизд**у**йте

Examples:

Пиздуй отсюда, урод! Get the fuck outta here, you freak!

Что делаешь? – Да вот, на работу пиздую. What are you up to now? – Here, on my fucking why to work.

Ну что, попиздовали домой? So what, let's fucking go home?

Пиздюх**а**ть (куда-то топать, куда-то направляться)

1) to walk somewhere, to hoof

Present

Я пиздюх**а**ю   Мы пиздюх**а**ем

Ты пиздюх**а**ешь   Вы пиздюх**а**ете

Он пиздюх**а**ет   Они пиздюх**а**ют

Past   ### Adverb

Он пиздюх**а**л   Пиздюх**а**я

Она пиздюх**а**ла   ### Directive

Они пиздюх**а**ли   Пиздюх**а**й

                    Пиздюх**а**йте

Examples:

Вчера видел Майлка, когда он пиздюхал в сторону своего дома. I saw Michael yesterday, he was fucking walking home.

Попиздюхали отсюда. Let's get the fuck out of here.

Повы**ё**бываться (повыпендриваться)

1) to show off

Present

Я повы**ё**бываюсь   Мы повы**ё**бываемся

Ты повы**ё**бываешься   Вы повы**ё**бываетесь

Он повы**ё**бывается   Они повы**ё**бываются

Past   ### Adverb

Он повы**ё**бывался   –

Она повы**ё**бывалась   ### Directive

Они повы**ё**бывались   –

Examples:

Ну повыёбывался и хватит. Enough fucking showing off.

Почему ты так любишь повыёбываться в присутствии незнакомых людей? Why do you like fucking showing off so much in front of people you don't even know?

Подоср**а**ть

1) Make wise ass comments, mess with someone

Future

Я подоср**у**	Мы подоср**ё**м
Ты подоср**ё**шь	Вы подоср**ё**те
Он подоср**ё**т	Они подоср**у**т

Past   ### Adverb

Он подоср**а**л   –

Она подоср**а**ла   **Directive**

Они подоср**а**ли   Подоср**и**

Подоср**и**те

Examples:

Она вечно всем подсирает, хочет любой ценой казаться лучше. She always makes wise ass comments, because she wants to appear better than she is at any cost.

Я особо не обращал на него внимания, пока он мне не подосрал с моим повышением. Тут-то и раскрылась его натура. I didn't pay attention to him until he fucking messed with my promotion. This is when he revealed his nature.

Подсос**а**ть

1) To borrow some money, to lend

Future

Я подсос**у**	Мы подсос**ё**м
Ты подсос**ё**шь	Вы подсос**ё**те
Он подсос**ё**т	Они подсос**у**т

Past

Он подсос**а**л

Она подсос**а**ла

Они подсос**а**ли

Adverb

–

Directive

Подсос**и**

Подсос**и**те

Examples:

Пришлось подсосать у родителей до стипендии. Had to borrow some cash from my parents till I get my maintenance allowance.

Я сейчас на подсосе. I'm living on borrowed money right now.

Подъеб**а**ть

1) To play a joke with someone/mess with someone

Future

Я подъеб**у**	Мы подъеб**ё**м
Ты подеб**ё**шь	Вы подъеб**ё**те
Он подъеб**ё**т	Они подъеб**у**т

Past

Он подъеб**а**л

Она подъеб**а**ла

Они подъеб**а**ли

Adverb

–

Directive

Подъеб**и**

Подъеб**и**те

Examples:

Я сказал это, чтобы просто подъебать тебя. I just said it to fucking mess with you.

Ребята, вам не удастся меня подъебать. Guys you won't be able to fucking mess with me.

Давай позвоним ей и подъъбём, скажем, что тест отменили. Let's call and fucking mess with her telling they cancelled the test.

Попизд**е**ть (поговорить о чём-то)

1) to chat, to small talk

Future

Я попизж**у**	Мы попизд**и**м
Ты попизд**и**шь	Вы попизд**и**те
Он попизд**и**т	Они попизд**я**т

Past   Adverb

Он попизд**и**л   -

Она попизд**и**ла   **Directive**

Они попизд**и**ли   Попизд**и**

                             Попизд**и**те

Examples:

Вы пока тут попиздите, а я пока сгоняю в магазин. You guys fucking chat here, I'll drive to the store meanwhile.

Подружка, наконец-то встретимся с тобой, попиздим, вырьем по бокальчику красненького. My dear friend, finally we'll meet and fucking chat and have a glass of red wine.

Посрать (опорожниться (совершенный вид))

1) to take a crap, to shit

Future

Я посру́	Мы посрём
Ты посрёшь	Вы посрёте
Он посрёт	Они посру́т

Past

Он посра́л

Она посра́ла

Они посра́ли

Adverb

–

Directive

Посри́

Посри́те

Examples:

Ну что, посрали? Мы уже опаздываем, давайте быстрее!
So what, have you shitted guys? We're already late!

Если я сейчас не посру, то у меня потом болеть живот.
If I don't shit now, I'll have a stomach ache later.

Поссать (пописать)

1) to piss, to take a leak

Future

Я поссу	Мы поссым
Ты поссышь	Вы поссыте
Он поссыт	Они поссут

Past

Он поссал

Она поссала

Они поссали

Adverb

-

Directive

Поссы

Поссыте

Examples:

Ты проверил, ребёнок поссал или нет? Did you check if the kid has pissed or not?

Ну что, выходим? – Сейчас поссу и пойдём. So, going out or not? – Let me piss and we'll go out.

Приеб**а**т**ь**<u>ся</u>

1) To bother

Future

Я приеб**у**сь   Мы приеб**ё**мся

Ты приеб**ё**шься   Вы приеб**ё**тесь

Он приеб**ё**тся   Они приеб**у**тся

Past   #### Adverb

Он приеб**а**лся   –

Она приеб**а**лась   #### Directive

Они приеб**а**лись   Приеб**и**сь

                            Приеб**и**тесь

Examples:

Да что ж ты приебался ко мне!   Stop fucking bothering me!

Приебаться к кому-нибудь, похоже, твоё любимое занятие. Seems like fucking bothering someone is your favorite.

Продроч**и**ть

1) To masturbate, to jerk, to wack off

Future

Я продроч**у**	Мы продр**о**чим
Ты продр**о**чишь	Вы продр**о**чите
Он продр**о**чит	Они продр**о**чат

Past | ### Adverb

Он продроч**и**л	–
Она продроч**и**ла	**Directive**
Они продроч**и**ли	Продроч**и**
	Продроч**и**те

Examples:

Может лучше просто продрочить, а то лень затеивать все эти любовные игры. Maybe it's just easier to jerk off, I don't fell like playing all these love games.

Продрочу-ка я лучше перед поездочкой, а то не известно, повезёт мне или нет. I guess I'll just wack off before the trip, who knows if I get lucky or not.

Проеб**а**ть (ся)

1) To lose

2) To fuck up

Future

Я проеб**у**(сь)   Мы проеб**ё**м(ся)

Ты проеб**ё**шь(ся)   Вы проеб**ё**те(сь)

Он проеб**ё**т(ся)   Они проеб**у**т(ся)

Past   ### Adverb

Он проеб**а**л(ся)   –

Она проеб**а**ла(сь)   ### Directive

Они проеб**а**ли(сь)   Проеб**и**

                          Проеб**и**те

Examples:

В первый же день проебал всё, что заработал, в казино! On the very first day he fucking lost everything he had earned in a casino.

Проебать всё в карты просто позорно. It's a shame to just fuck it all up playing cards.

Если проебусь с этой сделкой – точно напьюсь. If I fuck up this deal, I'll definitely get drunk.

Просра́ть(ся)

1) To fuck up, to screw up, to lose smth, to piss away

2) To beat the shit out of someone

3) To be able to crap after a period of constipation

Future

Я   просру́(сь)   Мы просрём(ся)

Ты просрёшь(ся)   Вы просрёте(сь)

Он просрёт(ся)   Они просру́т(ся)

Past

Он просра́л(ся)

Она просра́ла(сь)

Они просра́ли(сь)

Adverb

–

Directive

Просри́(сь)

Просри́те(сь)

Examples:

Майкл опять просрал все деньги в казино. Again Michael fucking pissed away all of his money in a casino.

Спасибо современной ммедицине, одна таблетка и я просрался как собака. Thanks to the modern medicine, just one pill and I shit like a dog.

Я больше не буду тебе помогать, ты вечно просираешь все возможности. I won't help you anymore, you always fuck up every chance you get.

Проссать

1) To lose (out), play away, crap out

2) Have trouble understanding, misunderstand

Future

Я проссу	Мы проссым
Ты проссышь	Вы проссыте
Он проссыт	Они проссут

Past

Он проссал

Она проссала

Они проссали

Adverb

–

Directive

Проссы

Проссыте

Examples:

Я что-то никак не проссу, какого хрена тебе от меня надо? I can't understand shit on what the fuck do you want from me?

Проссать с таким счётом просто позорно. Тренер должен подать в отставку. It's just a shame to fucking lose with this score. The coach should resign.

Дай ему 100 баксов — он их в автоматы за пол часа проссыт. Just give him 100 bucks and he'll piss them away in slot machines in half an hour.

Я был в таком шоке, что мне сложно было проссать, что же происходило вокруг меня. I was so shocked I could hardly get what the fuck was happening around me.

Разъеб**а**ть (сломать что-то, испортить, разрушить)

1) to fuck up, to break something

Future

Я разъеб**у**	Мы разъеб**ё**м
Ты разъеб**ё**шь	Вы разъеб**ё**те
Он разъеб**ё**т	Они разъеб**у**т

Past

Он разъеб**а**л

Она разъеб**а**ла

Они разъеб**а**ли

Adverb

–

Directive

Разъеб**и**

Разъеб**и**те

Examples:

Я не могу поверить, что он разъебал свою новую тачку буквально через неделю. I can't believe he fucked up his new car basically within a week.

Я разъебу тебе рожу, если ты не заткнёшься прямо сейчас. I'll ruin your fucking face if you don't shut up right now.

Расху**я**рить (то же, что «разъебать»)

1) to ruin smth, to fuck up

Future

Я расху**я**рю   Мы расху**я**рим

Ты расху**я**ришь   Вы расху**я**рите

Он расху**я**рит   Они расху**я**рят

Past   Adverb

Он расху**я**рил   –

Она расху**я**рила   **Directive**

Они расху**я**рили   Расху**я**рь

                             Расху**я**рьте

Examples:

Эта дура в припадке бешенства расхуярила мне всю мебель в комнате. This idiot ruined all of my fucking furniture in the room during her tantrum.

Если мой муж узнает о том, что ты мне тут пишешь, он расхуярит тебе морду. If my husband learns the shit you're writing me here, he'll break your fucking face.

Расху**я**чить (то же, что «разъебать»)

1) to ruin smth, to fuck up

Future

Я расху**я**чу	Мы расху**я**чим
Ты расху**я**чишь	Вы расху**я**чите
Он расху**я**чит	Они расху**я**чат

Past | ### Adverb

Он расху**я**чил	-
Она расху**я**чила	**Directive**
Они расху**я**чили	Расху**я**чь
	Расху**я**чьте

Examples:

Сука, я тебе сейчас всю тачку расхуячу! Bitch, I'll ruin your fucking ride now!

Помнишь, ты дарил мне набор бокал для шампанского? Я уже расхуячила два из шести. Remember you gave me a set of champagne glasses as a present? I've already fucking broken two out of six.

Сосать (ся)

1) To suck, to blow, do a blowjob, suck off

2) To French kiss

Present

Я сосу(сь)   Мы сосём(ся)

Ты сосёшь(ся)   Вы сосёте(сь)

Он сосёт(ся)   Они сосут(ся)

Past

Он сосал(ся)

Она сосала(сь)

Они сосали(сь)

Adverb

Сося

Directive

Соси(сь)

Сосите(сь)

Examples:

Сосать сначала научитесь. First learn how to blow.

Поди-ка сосни хуйца. Why don't you just go suck it off.

Пришлось с ней расстаться, а то на днях увидел, как она сосалась с другим парнем. Had to break up with her, because I saw her fucking French kissing some other guy the other day.

Спизд**е**ть (проболтаться, сболтнуть лишнего; наврать)

1) to put one's foot in one's mouth;

2) to lie

Future

Я спизж**у**	Мы спизд**им**
Ты спизд**ишь**	Вы спизд**ите**
Он спизд**ит**	Они спизд**я**т

Past

Adverb

Он спизд**е**л	–
Она спизд**е**ла	**Directive**
Они спизд**е**ли	–

Examples:

Похоже, Иван спизднул лишнего. Придётся тебе теперь выпутывать из этой ситуации. It seems like Ivan fucking put his foot in his mouth. You'll have to get him off the hook now.

Я точно уверен, что она спиздела. Ну не может такого быть! I'm pretty sure she fucking lied to us. It just cannot be true!

Спиздить (украсть что-то)

1) to steal smth, to nick

Future

Я спизжу	Мы спиздим
Ты спиздишь	Вы спиздите
Он спиздит	Они спиздят

Past

Он спиздил

Она спиздила

Они спиздили

Adverb

–

Directive

Спизди

Спиздите

Examples:

Депутаты уже немерено денег у народа спиздили. Но им всё мало. Lawmakers have fucking stolen a lot of money from the people. But it's still not enough for them.

Вчера у меня в автобусе спиздили кошелек. Так что, ребята, будьте всегда начеку. Yesterday in the bus someone fucking snitched my wallet. So stay vigilant, guys.

Срать(ся)

1) To poop, take a crap, crap, shit

2) To argue/fight

Present

Я сру(сь)	Мы срём(ся)
Ты срёшь(ся)	Вы срёте(сь)
Он срётс(ся)	Они срут(ся)

Past

Adverb

Он срал(ся)	-
Она срала(сь)	**Directive**
Они срали(сь)	Сри(сь)
	Сりите(сь)

Examples:

Я не представляю, что буду делать, если мне приспичит срать во время поездки. I can't imagine what I would do if I feel an urge to shit during the trip.

Пока я срал, телефон разрывался от звонков. While I was taking a crap, the phone was ringing off the hook.

Эти двое постоянно срутся из-за всякой фигни. These two are constantly fighting because of some nonsense.

Мне надоело сраться со своими друзьями из-за того, что ты вечно никуда не хочешь идти. I'm sick and tired of fighting with my friends because you never want to go out anywhere.

94

Ссать(ся)

1) To piss, to pee
2) Get off on (for a strong positive emotion)
3) To be afraid, to be scared, to be nervous

Present

Я ссу(сь)	Мы ссым(ся)
Ты ссышь(ся)	Вы ссыте(сь)
Он ссыт(ся)	Они ссут(ся)

Past

Он ссал(ся)

Она ссала(сь)

Они ссали(сь)

Adverb

—

Directive

Ссы(сь)

Ссыте(сь)

Examples:

Мне надо срочно поссать. Остановите машину. I need to take a piss urgently. Stop the car.

После той драки я неделю ссал кровью. After that fight I pissed blood for a week.

Съеб**а**ть (ся)

1) To get lost, to get the fuck out

Future

Я съеб**у**(сь)	Мы съеб**ё**м(ся)
Ты съеб**ё**шь(ся)	Вы съеб**ё**те(сь)
Он съеб**ё**т(ся)	Они съеб**у**т(ся)

Past

Он съеб**а**л(ся)

Она съеб**а**ла(сь)

Они съеб**а**ли(сь)

Adverb

Съеб**а**вши(сь)

Directive

Съеб**и**(сь)

Съеб**и**те(сь)

Examples:

А ну-ка быстро все съебались отсюда! Hey everyone, get the fuck outta here!

Съебаться из этой дыры не так-то просто. It's not that simple to get the fuck outta this shithole.

Съебись с глаз моих долой! Just get fucking lost!

Съёбывать(ся) (откуда-то убегать, уходить (быстро))

1) to to get the fuck out, to flee, to run away

Present

Я съёбываю(сь)   Мы съёбываем(ся)

Ты съёбываешь(ся)   Вы съёбываете(сь)

Он съёбывают(ся)   Они съёбывают(ся)

Past   ### Adverb

Он съёбывал(ся)   -

Она съёбывала(ся)   ### Directive

Они съёбыывали(сь)   Съёбывай(ся)

                        Съёбывайте(сь)

Examples:

Я не знаю как вы, а я заканчиваю университет и съёбываю нафиг из этого города. I'm not sure about you guys, but I'll graduate from college and get the fuck out of this town.

Быстро съёбывайся отсюда, пока тебя не увидели менты! Flee the fuck away, 'till the cops don't see you!

Тр**а**хать(ся)

1) To fuck, to bang

2) To fuck with someone

Present

Я тр**а**хаю(сь)	Мы тр**а**хаем(ся)
Ты тр**а**хаешь(ся)	Вы тр**а**хаете(сь)
Он тр**а**хает(ся)	Они тр**а**хают(ся)

Past

Он тр**а**хал(ся)

Она тр**а**хала(сь)

Они тр**а**хали(сь)

Adverb

Тр**а**хая(сь)

Directive

Тр**а**хни(сь)

Тр**а**хните(сь)

Examples:

Я две недели трахался с этим отчётом, а теперь он ему не нужен! I've been fucking with this report for two weeks, and now he doesn't need it!

С удовольствием трахнул бы эту тёлочку. I would love to fuck this hot chick.

Он трахает всё что движется. He fucks anything that moves.

Уганд**о**шить (кого-то побить; что-то разбить, испортить)

1) to beat the crap out of someone
2) to wreck smth

Future

Я угранд**о**шу	Мы угранд**о**шим
Ты угранд**о**шишь	Вы угранд**о**шите
Он угранд**о**шит	Они угранд**о**шат

Past   ### Adverb

Он угранд**о**шил   –

Она угранд**о**шила   **Directive**

Они угранд**о**шили   –

Examples:

Я тебя сейчас угандошу, если ты не заткнёшь свой поганый рот. I'll fucking beat the crap out of you right now if you don't shut your disgusting mouth.

Майкл купил у меня мою старую тачку. Так он за неделю её угандошил так, как я за 3 года не сумел. Michael bought my old car. He fucking wrecked it up in a week more than I managed to in 3 years.

Уеб**а**ть

1) To hit someone, to smash, to beat the shit out of

Future

Я уеб**у**	Мы уеб**ё**м
Ты уеб**ё**шь	Вы уеб**ё**те
Он уеб**ё**т	Они уеб**у**т

Past   ### Adverb

Он уеб**а**л   –

Она уеб**а**ла   ### Directive

Они уеб**а**ли   Уеб**и**

Уеб**и**те

Examples:

Слышишь, сука, сейчас как уебу! Hey bitch, I'm gonna beat the shit outta you!

Этот придурок уебал мне прямо в грёбаную челюсть. This meathead hit me right in my fucking jaw.

Уёбывать (куда-то сваливать, спешно уходить или сбегать; отвалить)

1) to get away, get out

Present

Я уёбываю	Мы уёбываем
Ты уёбываешь	Вы уёбываете
Он уёбывает	Они уёбывают

Past   ### Adverb

Он уебнул   –

Она уебнула   ### Directive

Они уебнули   Уёбывай

Уёбывайте

Examples:

А ну-ка уёбывай отсюда! Yo, get the fuck out of here!

Я не знаю как вы, но я свою жопу поднимаю и уёбываю. Not sure about you guys, but I'm raising my ass and getting the fuck away from here.

Усос**а**ть

1) To drink, to have a drink/bottle
2) To suck, to suck in

Future

Я усос**у**	Мы усос**ё**м
Ты усос**ё**шь	Вы усос**ё**те
Он усос**ё**т	Они усос**у**т

Past   Adverb

Он усос**а**л   –

Она усос**а**ла   **Directive**

Они усос**а**ли   Усос**и**

                     Усос**и**те

Examples:

Усосали бутылку виски за пол часа. They fucking drank a bottle of whiskey in half an hour.

Усосите, лузеры.   Suck it, losers.

Усосем-ка по пивку.   Let's fucking drink some beer.

Усра́ться

1) To shit in the pants, to be afraid of smth

2) To laugh your ass off

3) Put your foot down

Future

Я усру́сь	Мы усрёмся
Ты усрёшься	Вы усрётесь
Он усрётся	Они усру́тся

Past

Он усра́лся

Она усра́лась

Они усра́лись

Adverb

–

Directive

Усри́сь

Усри́тесь

Examples:

Огромная змея заползла ночью на террасу. Я усрался просто! A huge snake crawled in the terrace during the night. I just shit my pants!

Мы усрались с его историй, ему надо бы книгу приключений написать. We laughed our fucking asses off listening to his stories, he should write an adventure book.

Я усрался от страха, когда спросонья мне показалось, что в моей комнате кто-то стоит. I shit my pants when I was half-awake and thought someone was standing in my room.

Усс**а**ться   (сильно смеяться над чем-то)

1) to piss oneself (laughing)

Future

Я усс**у**ссь	Мы усс**ы**мся
Ты усс**ы**шься	Вы усс**ы**тесь
Он усс**ы**тся	Они усс**у**тся

Past   ### Adverb

Он усс**а**лся   –

Она усс**а**лась   ### Directive

Они усс**а**лись   Усс**ы**сь

                           Усс**ы**тесь

Examples:

Я уссался над этой книгой. Обязательно прочти её! I pissed myself reading this book. You should definitely read it!

Если в гости прийдёт Миша, все просто уссутся со смеху. If Michael comes along, everyone will just piss themselves laughing.

Уссыв**а**ться (то же, что "уссаться", но более продолжительное действие)

1) piss one's pants with laughter, be in fits of laughter

Present

Я уссыв**а**юсь	Мы уссыв**а**емся
Ты уссыв**а**ешься	Вы уссыв**а**етесь
Он уссыв**а**ется	Они уссыв**а**ются

Past

Он уссыв**а**лся

Она уссыв**а**лась

Они уссыв**а**лись

Adverb

–

Directive

Уссыв**а**йся

Уссыв**а**йтесь

Examples:

Как фильм? – Отличный! Мы всю дорогу уссывались со смеху. How was the movie? – Great! We've been pissing ourselves laughing on the way back.

Дети вообще смешные создания. Уссываются со смеху над любой глупостью. Kids are funny creatures. They piss their pants with laughter on any silliness.

Ху**и** пин**а**ть (заниматься ничегонеделаньем. Иногда употребляется просто как «пинать»)

1) to spend time doing nothing

Present

Я ху**и** пин**а**ю	Мы ху**и** пин**а**ем
Ты ху**и** пин**а**ешь	Вы ху**и** пин**а**ете
Он ху**и** пин**а**ет	Они ху**и** пин**а**ют

Past   ### Adverb

Он ху**и** пин**а**л   —

Она ху**и** пин**а**ла   ### Directive

Они ху**и** пин**а**ли   —

Examples:

Хватит хуи пинать! Пойди уже найди себе работу. Stop fucking around doing nothing! Go get yourself a job.

Пока в универе все хуи пинали, я учился и вкалывал на двух работах. While everyone in college was fucking hanging out and doing nothing, I was studying plus slaving on two jobs.

Ху**я**чить (кого-то бить, куда-то идти, что-то делать/чем-то заниматься)

    1) to hit, to beat someone
    2) to walk somewhere, to hoof
    3) to be doing something

Present

Я хуя́чу	Мы хуя́чим
Ты хуя́чишь	Вы хуя́чите
Он хуя́чит	Они хуя́чят

Past
Он хуя́чил
Она хуя́чила
Они хуя́чили

Adverb
Хуя́ча

Directive
Хуя́чь
Хуя́чьте

Examples:

Целый день хуячила по дому: погладила, постирала. Устала как собака. Been fucking slaving at home all day long: did the laundry and the ironing. I'm tired to the bone.

Он сказал, что не сможет меня туда отвезти. Придётся самой туда хуячить, потеряю часа два времени. He told me he wouldn't be able to ride me there. I'll have to drag there myself, will have to spend at least two hours on that.

Последние новости: этого козла отхуячили вчера. Нам тут гандоны не нужны. Latest news: the guys fucking beat the crap out of that ass yesterday. We don't need any douchebags here.

(За)Чмор**и**ть (унижать кого-то, затюкивать, оскорблять)

1) to insult, to bully, to denigrate

Present

Я чмор**ю**	Мы чмор**им**
Ты чмор**ишь**	Вы чмор**ите**
Он чмор**ит**	Они чмор**ят**

Past

Он чмор**ил**

Она чмор**ила**

Они чмор**или**

Adverb

–

Directive

–

Examples:

Хватит чморить бедного ребёнка! Так он вообще ничего не выучит! Stop fucking bullying the poor kid! This way he won't ever learn anything!

Ты его посмоянно чморишь. Он скоро от тебя сбежит. You always fucking denigrate him. He'll run away from you very soon.

Шмал**и**ть (курить траву, курить сигареты)

1) smoke weed (mostly) or smoke cigarettes)

Present

Я   шмал**ю**   Мы шмал**и**м

Ты шмал**ишь**   Вы шмал**и**те

Он шмал**и**т   Они шмал**я**т

Past   ### Adverb

Он шмал**и**л   —

Она шмал**и**ла   ### Directive

Они шмал**и**ли   Пошмал**и**

                            Пошмал**и**те

Examples:

Есть чё пошмалить? Got something to smoke?

Да эта баба шмалит как паровоз! Больше любого мужика.
Bitch smokes like a train! More than any guy.

Шп**и**лить (заниматься сексом/совокупляться, куда-то идти/топать)

1) to screw

Present

Я шп**и**лю	Мы шп**и**лим
Ты шп**и**лишь	Вы шп**и**лите
Он шп**и**лит	Они шп**и**лят

Past

Он шп**и**лил

Она шп**и**лила

Они шп**и**лили

Adverb

Шп**и**ля

Directive

(По)Шп**и**ль

(По)Шп**и**льте

Examples:

Было время, шпилили девок направо и налево. There was a time when we screwed girls right and left.

Не могла у метро поймать такси, пришлось пешком шпилить до дома. Couldn't get a taxi at the metro station, so had to hoof home all by myself.

Эх, пошпилить бы кого-нибудь сейчас! Heh, would like to screw someone right now!

Made in the USA
Columbia, SC
26 March 2025

55704760R00061